The Layman's Guide to Whelping Puppies – From Conception to New Home

By
Karen J Cornwell

Breeding a litter of puppies can be a very rewarding and enjoyable experience but it can also be traumatic if things don't go according to plan.

This book is intended to guide the novice breeder step-by-step through the whole process with a few tips included to help your new puppy owners through the puppy training phase.

Cover Photograph Courtesy of Mrs T Bell
(Windstream Whippets) U.K

www.windstreamwhippetscom.webden.co.uk

"There is no psychiatrist in the world like a puppy licking your face..."

~ Ben Williams

Contents

Introduction

This book is intended to guide you through your first experience of Dog Breeding. It is NOT intended as a substitute for Veterinary Care
If you have any concerns AT ALL please always contact your Veterinary Practice

Note: **Before you even consider breeding a litter of puppies, you should make sure that the dog and bitch that you intend to breed from are excellent examples of their breed.**

Think carefully about the implications of caring for the puppies properly before finding top class homes for *every one*.

There are enough unwanted dogs in the world and you do not want to add to that number.

Breed selectively and carefully to make sure that none of your puppies end up in the Dog Shelter with no-one to love him!

IMPORTANT

This Book is a General Guide and is *Not* Breed Specific. You Should Do Some Careful Research to Determine any Common Whelping Problems That May be Associated with Your Breed.

"Anybody who doesn't know what soap tastes like has never washed a dog..."
~Franklin P. Jones

Why do you want to Breed a Litter of Puppies?

You may have a bitch that has been very successful in her field, whether it is showing, agility, field trials, racing etc. and want to carry on the bloodlines and breed a litter for the future.

That is great and in my opinion, the only reason to have a litter of puppies.

You will still need to give the idea a lot of thought before you make a final decision and the questions on the next page are intended to help you with that decision.

Consider this...

- Have you got a list of people waiting for a puppy out of your bitch?

- Will you have good homes for all the puppies - there may be 10 in a litter? If no-one wants your breeding, why would you want a litter?

- Could you keep the puppies if some remain unsold?

- Are you prepared to give up three months of your life to care for your pregnant bitch and her puppies?

- Have you got an appropriate place that can be set aside for the bitch and her puppies for at least ten weeks?

- Will you have the time to care for the bitch and her puppies properly? It is a huge commitment and takes time and dedication to do the job properly.

- Could you cope in an emergency situation?

- Could you cope with the trauma if your bitch had a malformed or stillborn puppy?

- Do you have enough money to be able to pay for an unexpected Veterinary bill in the event of complications? A caesarean section is not cheap!

- Do you have enough money available for the stud fee, puppy registration fees, wormers, parasite treatments and Veterinary visits pre and post natal?

- Do you have enough money to provide the very best of everything for the bitch and her puppies?

If you can not answer 'Yes' to every one of the above questions then you should not even consider breeding a litter of puppies.

If you are still determined to breed from your fantastic bitch then read on…

The Bitch

One of the most important factors in successfully breeding a great litter of puppies is the health and suitability of both the sire and the bitch.

- Is your bitch an *exceptional* example of the breed? Has she excelled in her field of expertise? The fact that she is a great pet is not a good enough reason to breed from her.

- Does she have a great temperament? No-one wants to breed (or sell) puppies with uncertain or nervous temperaments.

- Is she in great health? Pregnancy and birth will take a lot out of your bitch and she needs to be in great shape to start off with.

Once you have determined that your bitch has everything that you would want to pass on to her puppies, you need to look carefully at choosing the right sire to father the new babies.

Choosing a Sire

This decision should be made well in advance of your girl coming into season.

When selecting a sire to father your new puppies, it is important to take note of certain traits that appear in his progeny. Ask if you can meet the prospective sire and some of his puppies.

A reputable stud dog owner will be delighted to show off his stud dog and tell you about the successes of his stud dog's progeny.

Some sires have a tendency to consistently produce puppies with excellent conformation, soundness and genuine, honest temperaments.

Obviously, such traits are highly desirable in any puppy.

Similarly, some sires have a tendency to produce the opposite and it is crucial that the potential breeder pay attention to these factors.

Given the expense of breeding a litter and the need to produce good, healthy puppies that are a good example of their breed type; it is important to avoid bloodlines notorious for producing poor traits.

You should avoid sires that have produced inherited breed specific diseases, uncertain temperament or poor conformation in their progeny.

Does your breed have any specific problems that may be passed to the puppies?

There are some breeds that are predisposed to hip or eye problems; **have you checked for any specific problems inherent in your breed?**

Some breeds may also have aesthetic requirements. The Rhodesian Ridgeback for example, may be born without a ridge, with more than two perfectly positioned whorls or with a crooked ridge. Anything other than a perfect ridge would exclude that puppy from the show ring, so would you be able to find him a permanent loving home if this happened?

Would you be able to find good pet homes for any puppies that do not meet the required breed standard?

If you are not sure which stud keeper to approach, ask around within your breed circle – a good recommendation is worth its weight in gold.

Is She in Season?

Bitches come in season or 'on heat' at different times.

Each one is different.

Some have six month cycles whilst others have eighteen month cycles. Most bitches will have at least one season a year.

When you decide to enter the breeding arena, you should begin to keep some records of your potential brood bitch's cycle, so that you will know approximately when to expect her next season.

Be guided by the Kennel Club in your country regarding the accepted age to breed from your bitch. Over two years old is a general guide. Give your bitch time to be a puppy herself before making her a Mom.

When she is approaching the time when your records show that she is due in season, watch her carefully. Take a piece of white toilet tissue and dab her vulva each morning before she goes out to do her toilet.

When you start to see a coloring on the tissue, make a note of the date. Some bitches will only show a slight staining for a day or two whilst others will bleed profusely for around two weeks.

You will know what to expect from your bitch if you have kept records from previous seasons.

As soon as you notice the first staining, contact your chosen stud keeper to let him know that your bitch has begun her season. He will be able to advise on the best time to arrive at the stud for her to be mated.

A good sign that she is ready to be mated:

If you scratch her back near the base of her tail it will immediately go off to the side and she will stand with her back legs slightly apart.

The usual time for a bitch to be mated is around 14 days from the onset of the bleeding – but again, all bitches are different. Some will be ready earlier and some a lot later. You could have her progesterone levels tested to determine if she is ovulating to give you the very best chance of a successful mating.

What if She Doesn't Come in Season?

If you have a bitch that has never had a season at all by around two years old, it may be a good idea to have her checked out by your Vet.

However, if you are waiting for a bitch to come in season that has previously had a normal season and she is a little late; in order to speed things up you could try moving her to a different kennel.

If you know someone who has a bitch in season, try kennelling them together.

If she is a house dog, try booking her into a boarding kennel for a couple of days.

A change of surroundings can sometimes help bring a bitch in season. This has worked well for me. My girl usually comes in season when we go on holiday and are staying in hotels with crisp white sheets…

Your Vet also has an injection called Galastop at his disposal that could help. There is no guarantee, but it could be worth a try. It will however, mean daily injections until she comes in season and should be a last resort.

Be vigilant when she does come in season.

If your bitch is mated by accident, a trip to the Vet at the earliest opportunity for an injection will make sure that she doesn't end up pregnant by the neighbors mixed breed.

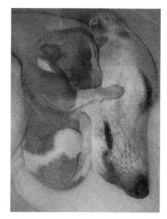

Whippet Mother and one of her new babies

Windstream Whippets

The Mating

It is usual to take the bitch to the stud dog for mating. But these days, there are other ways to achieve the same thing.

There are three types of stud service available:

1. Natural Mating

This is where the stud dog physically mates the bitch. In this case your bitch will be taken to the kennels where the stud dog is kept as most stud dogs 'work' better when they are on familiar ground.

The stud keeper will advise you at what stage in her cycle to bring her to his kennel. With a natural mating only one bitch can be mated at a time, the sperm cannot be examined for quality and the bitch will receive the whole ejaculate.

She would usually be mated twice, two days apart to give her the best chance of becoming pregnant. If your chosen stud dog is a long way from your home, your bitch may have to stay at the stud keepers kennel for a week or so. Alternatively you could arrange to stay over somewhere close so that you can take your bitch back for the second mating. That will be something that you should discuss with the stud keeper in advance.

2. Artificial Insemination (A.I.)

This is where the semen is taken from the dog, analyzed for quality, and then inserted into one or more bitches depending on the volume and quality of sperm produced.

It is usually inserted in a narrow tube into the bitch in order for the semen to travel to the uterus, or by endoscope which will insert the semen directly into the uterus.

3. Frozen Semen Insemination

This is where the semen is collected as in A.I. except in this case the semen is frozen for use at a later date (it could be two days, two weeks, two years or ten years from now). Once the semen is collected it is then analysed for volume, quality and abnormality.

Frozen semen is surgically implanted in the uterus of the bitch under anesthetic.

The main reason for this is that frozen semen only lives for 24 to 36 hours and the semen is unlikely to live long enough to fertilize the bitch if administered by A.I.

The advantage of frozen semen is that it makes it possible for a bitch in one part of the world to be mated to a stud dog from another part of the world without any travelling involved.

Is She Pregnant?

If you are uncertain if your bitch is pregnant, it is a good idea to have her scanned by your Vet at around 5/6 weeks, not only to determine if she is, in fact, pregnant but also the probable size of the litter.

Over-feeding a bitch that is only having 1 or 2 puppies could potentially create the problem of a small litter being very large puppies.

This could make delivering these large puppies vaginally a problem for the bitch, which could mean that a planned Caesarian section would be necessary.

A Healthy Pregnant Greyhound - 7 weeks into pregnancy

She had a Surgical Insemination – you can see the shaved area where the tiny incision was made.

First Signs of Pregnancy

You may notice that the bitch will start to 'look after' herself. Instead of leaping around you may find that she will become a bit calmer, this could happen at around two to three weeks into the pregnancy. This may not be noticeable in a lot of bitches. However, if you know your bitch well, it will be easier to spot these slight changes in her behavior.

Her teats may become more prominent and a little 'pinker' and the hair around the nipples is not as thick as before. This is usually most noticeable in maiden (has not had puppies before) bitches.

Some, but not all, will go off their food for a day or two around three weeks after they have been mated.

She may even vomit at this stage. It is usually a yellow froth or bile and is probably nothing more than 'morning sickness'. However, check her temperature at this time to make sure that the sickness is not caused by any underlying infection.

In some bitches you may not see any sign of pregnancy until it is nearly time for whelping. If you are at all unsure if your bitch is pregnant, you should schedule an ultrasound scan so your Vet can tell you if there are any puppies inside her.

Exercise

The amount of exercise that a pregnant bitch should receive is very much a balancing act.

It important that the bitch does not become a couch potato; there is no need to stop her daily walks. But try and avoid any rough and tumble play to avoid any risk of her aborting or damaging the unborn puppies during the early weeks of her pregnancy.

She should have controlled exercise as long as she still wants to; this will keep her muscles toned which will help her deal with the strain of giving birth.

Early Pregnancy

Your bitch's pregnancy will last from between 58 and 64 days following mating.

How she is looked after during this time is absolutely crucial to producing a strong, healthy and thriving litter. Management will vary at different stages depending on nutritional or other requirements.

It is ideal if the bitch is very slightly (5%) overweight at the time of mating so that she can sustain a slight loss of weight during mating.

This would be particularly relevant if she has to go away from home to be mated as some bitches will refuse to eat for a day or two when they are in unfamiliar surroundings.

Correct nutrition contributes a lot to the breeding success and it is important to consider this carefully. Puppies are unlikely to recover from a bad start if poor nutrition of the bitch leads to poor development in the womb.

Nutritional needs mostly depend on the stage of the pregnancy and the litter size.

During the reproductive process the bitch's diet must support three areas:

1. Her body maintenance
2. The growth of her reproductive tissues
3. The growth and development of her unborn puppy.

Ultimately, the puppies will take what they need via the placenta. If the bitch is not adequately fed, her body fat reserves and body tissues may be broken down to maintain the puppies that are growing inside her.

The goal, therefore, is to produce a healthy litter of puppies whilst maintaining the health and condition of the bitch.

4 weeks old

What to Feed

It is a good idea to increase the bitch's food slightly immediately after mating, as a lot will go off their food for a couple of days at around two weeks into their pregnancy.

In the early stages of pregnancy, the bitch's nutritional requirements are similar to that of a normal maintenance diet.

So, as long as she has always been fed a **good quality feed**, you should continue to feed her what she is used to.

However, it may be a good idea to gradually introduce other things to her diet as she may well go off her usual feeds. For example, sardines in vegetable oil, milk and cereal, scrambled eggs etc. can be used to tempt a bitch who is off her food.

Do not be tempted to give a calcium supplement before the birth.

This could cause the body's natural production of calcium to be interrupted. Her needs should be met by simply feeding a good quality feed.

If the bitch was in first class condition (and she should have been!) before mating then from early pregnancy up to week 6 her normal diet will be acceptable.

For the final three weeks of gestation however, the unborn puppies start to grow very fast. At this time the bitch will require appropriate feeding to maintain her own health and the health of the unborn puppies.

The Final Three Weeks – What to Feed

As long as you are confident that she is, in fact, in whelp, you should aim to increase the bitch's food intake from around week 6 or 7.

Her feed should be divided into smaller feeds and given throughout the day. Little and often will ensure that she gets a comfortable feeding regime.

From week 6 or 7, in addition to her normal feeds, I also make sure there is always dry food (kibble) available to her so she can pick at it throughout the day.

Even the very greedy mother-to-be will usually regulate her own intake at this time as she will not have room in her abdomen for a huge amount of food. But you should use your own judgement to determine if this is the right approach for your bitch.

As a matter of course, make sure that the bitch has access to plenty of **fresh, clean** drinking water at all times.

It is important that the bitch has enough food to keep herself and her rapidly growing litter in a good healthy condition until weaning.

A further increase in food intake will be necessary when the puppies are about 3 weeks old, when lactation is at its most demanding.

Again, my personal solution to this is to allow her free access to dry food in addition to her normal feeds.

Greyhound – 8 weeks pregnant

She will usually just want to sit or lie around at this stage.

Parasite Control for the Pregnant Bitch

Worming

Worming is another very important factor in producing a healthy litter of puppies.

Your bitch should be wormed with a suitable wormer and treated for any external parasites **before** going to be mated.

The problem with worms is that they are never totally eliminated no matter how diligent the owner is. In addition, the stress of the pregnancy allows the worm burden to grow.

Worm the pregnant bitch again 5 weeks into her pregnancy with a safe and proven wormer. Worming any earlier may be harmful to the puppies that are still forming in the womb.

If you are at all unsure as to what is a safe product for worming the mother-to-be, please ask your Vet.

It is **VERY IMPORTANT** to ensure that your bitch is well wormed as it helps minimize the worm burden that will inevitably be transferred to her puppies through her milk.

External Parasites

Before going to be mated, your bitch should have been completely free from external parasites. If she does have any fleas or whatever, you should take steps to eradicate them before the puppies are born.

Speak to your Vet who will advise you on a safe treatment for the pregnant bitch.

Make sure that your bitch's vaccinations are up to date before mating. This will ensure that the puppies will be protected by the bitch's antibodies during the first few weeks of their life.

Whippet puppies of

Barnesmore Gypsy Rose at Oaksmoorehill

Preparation

It is important to be well prepared for the birth as it is not unknown for the bitch to give birth a few days earlier than expected. I had a bitch that gave birth to 9 healthy puppies 6 days early.

So, be prepared to hang around for the week before the due date – just in case!

No day trips or weekends away at this time.

A decision must be made as soon as you know that your bitch is pregnant as to where she will be having her puppies.

A whelping box in a quiet area is very important.

The new mother will need privacy and quiet to care for her new babies.

If you are planning to have puppies more than once, you can buy or make a wooden whelping box that should have sides low enough for the bitch to jump in and out, but high enough to keep the puppies in.

Put a hinged flap at the front that can be dropped to provide a ramp for when the puppies are ready to leave the bed and explore.

This whelping box should be ***thoroughly cleaned and disinfected*** before and after every use.

There are some fantastic whelping boxes available that are easily cleaned and will dismantle for easy storage.

Another cheaper solution for a 'one time only' litter of puppies is a whelping box made from strong cardboard.

These can be disposed of once you have finished with them.

Again, these are widely available online.

If you are planning for the birth to take place in an outside kennel; a heat lamp will be essential (even in summer in some countries) to keep your puppies warm. Puppies are very fragile and cold and draughts could easily kill your new babies.

Another necessity, if your whelping area is in an outside kennel, is a good light source so you can see what is going on, as most bitches will have their babies at night.

Before moving your bitch to the whelping area, it is crucial to make sure that you thoroughly clean the whole area. Use a disinfectant that has good anti-bacterial and anti-viral properties.

Once the whelping area has been set up, it can be lined with newspapers which are then covered with a suitable bedding material.

Some breeders use newspaper for the bedding itself; but this is not very comfortable and can be slippery and will provide little traction for a heavily pregnant bitch who is trying to reach round to her newborn puppy to chew the cord.

Carpet tiles provide excellent traction and can be secured to the floor of the bed. They dry quickly and can be pulled up and replaced after each whelping.

My own personal preference is VetBed™ on top of newspapers; this is a sheepskin-like fabric which allows the liquid to seep through to be soaked up by the newspaper whilst the bedding stays relatively dry. It is easy to obtain and is quick and easy to wash and dry and will last a long time.

Picture:

Well-used & well-washed VetBed™

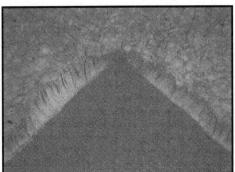

A duvet or blankets is not a good idea as the bitch will sometimes dig at the bedding and inadvertently bury one or two of the tiny puppies.

Moving the bitch to the whelping box is best done gradually. Dogs are pack animals and removing a pregnant bitch from the security of her family could be stressful.

The best way is to introduce her to the whelping area for an hour or so each day in the 14 days up to the due date of her litter and then totally at the end of the pregnancy when she has just 3 or 4 days to go.

All she really wants to do then is to lie down and rest.

You may notice that the bitch has severe swelling of the legs and feet and is often very swollen around the vulva. This is usually nothing to worry about and as soon as the bitch has given birth this will disappear.

It would be a good idea to allow her constant access to a yard or somewhere that she can walk around to relieve the pressure if she feels like it.

8 weeks pregnant

Useful Supplies for the Birth

Here is a list of supplies that could be useful during the birth:

Thermometer – for monitoring the temperature of the bitch prior to whelping (it usually falls below normal about 24 hours before she will whelp).

Accurate Scales – that weigh in grams, for weighing the puppies. Birth weights vary according to breed (check yours) but regular monitoring of weights is a good way to ensure the puppies are thriving.

Scissors (blunt) – for cutting umbilical cords if the bitch fails to do it. The bitch will 'crush' the cord with her teeth. So you should try to imitate this action if necessary. I would usually break the cord with my (clean) fingernails if the bitch doesn't do it. It is very tough, but you should never make a clean cut as it makes it easier for infection to enter.

Dental Floss – for tying off an umbilical cord that keeps bleeding.

Clean boiled towels – for drying the puppies off if the bitch fails to do it. I have about 20 towelling tea towels that I keep especially for this. They are boiled after each use in readiness for the next litter.

Garbage bags – for wet, soiled newspaper bedding and other rubbish.

Disinfectant – for the hands; preferably non-scented. It is important not to introduce alien smells onto the puppies.

Dopram – This is a product which stimulates the breathing reflex. A couple of drops under the tongue will help a puppy that is slow to breathe, particularly the later born ones. This is available from your Vet.

CCTV – A great help to both breeder and bitch. They are cheap and cheerful these days and very simple to install (even I can do it!). It means that the bitch is not disturbed until it is time to assist her – no running in and out to see how she is – just watch the screen.

Surgical spirits - for the cord if necessary – doesn't smell.

A bucket with a lid – for stillborn puppies or placentas.

Clean Bedding – For when all the puppies have been born and the bitch is settling down to care for her new babies.

Dishes for the bitch – she may appreciate a drink during labor.

Box for Puppies – Useful for if the puppies need to be away from the bitch whilst she delivers more puppies. A small laundry basket containing a heat source covered with VetBed™ is a good solution. It is easy to carry when it is time for the Vet to see the bitch and puppies.

Veterinary Telephone Number – It is very important to have a Vet available on call if needed, particularly if you are inexperienced.

Make sure that you have transport (with a full fuel tank) available during the birth as you may need to go to the Veterinary surgery in a hurry should any problems arise.

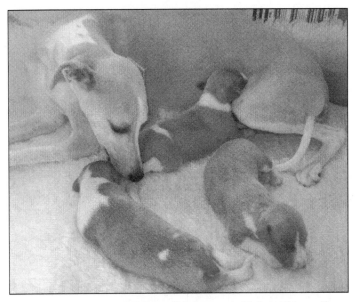

Beautiful Whippet Mother doing a great job looking after her new babies

Windstream Whippets

Signs that the Birth is Imminent

Once the bitch has been mated there will be an expected date of whelping, which will be roughly 63 days from the time of ovulation and insemination. It could be a week either side but generally, 63-64 days is normal.

The normal temperature for a dog is 38.9° to 39.7° C (100.9° to 101.7° F). To check her temperature use a stubby thermometer and a suitable lubricant, insert it gently into her anus (you may need someone to hold her) and wait for the required amount of time.

Take her temperature a few times at around 6 weeks then you know what her normal temperature is.

Then, a few days before her due date, you could begin to take her temperature every six hours or so. It is normal for the bitch's temperature to drop below 37.8° C (100° F) approximately 24 hours before giving birth.

This method is useful but not infallible, to determine when she will give birth.

You may notice a string of mucus hanging from the vulva; this is the 'plug' that has detached from the neck of the uterus in preparation for the birth. She will usually have her puppies within 24-36 hours.

Many bitches will go off their food just before the birth and most will become restless. They will often scrape and tear at their bedding while panting heavily whilst their body is preparing to deliver the puppies.

Occasionally some bitches may remain calm and continue eating, but this an exception.

If there is a concern that the bitch has gone over her due date without any signs of the puppies arriving, or a caesarean section has been planned, testing the blood progesterone level can be carried out by the Vet to determine if the bitch is ready to deliver the puppies.

Progesterone levels will drop considerably at the time of birth. Your Vet can test to determine if it is the right time to carry out a caesarean.

Signs that things are not progressing normally

Note: Knowing the warning signs is crucial to determine if there is a problem or whether the pregnancy is progressing normally.

A Vet should be on call in case Veterinary intervention is necessary.

- **Black or dark green discharge before a puppy has arrived - ALWAYS** consult the Vet. Placentas may be deteriorating or puppies may be dead.

- **Uterine inertia** - This is where the uterus fails to contract. You would notice a large floppy belly as the bitch is lying down. Usually, as the whelping day draws near the uterus 'tightens' and its outline can be seen on both sides of the bitch's flanks – obviously this is easier to see on a short coated breed.

Uterine inertia could be hereditary or more likely there is a huge litter of puppies and no contractions are possible. Alternatively the bitch may have had too many litters and the uterus is 'used up' and tired.

In both of the above circumstances a Caesarean Section is usually necessary.

If you are concerned about anything during the pregnancy or birth, consult your Veterinary Surgeon immediately.

It may save the lives of both your bitch and the puppies.

Labour – First Stage

At this stage the bitch will usually become quite restless. She may begin panting heavily and shivering uncontrollably.

- This is normal.

The bitch's body is preparing to whelp but contractions are not yet visible. It is not unusual for a bitch to vomit at this stage and for that vomit to be no more than froth.

- This is nothing to be concerned about.

You may see some small, infrequent contractions; this is her body lining up the puppies in the birth canal for delivery. You **WILL** know the difference between these and a full blown contraction.

The bitch should now be in the whelping area or she may have her puppies elsewhere.

Some bitches, particularly older ones, may hide at this stage so it is important that she is unable to get into some other place where she may be difficult to get to.

In my early days of breeding, I let one of my brood bitches, who was due to whelp and panting heavily, out into the garden to 'empty'.

I went inside to do something thinking she would come back in when she had finished. When I looked outside a minute later there was no sign of her!

I found her 10 minutes later making a 'nest' in the straw in the corner of a stable. That was a lesson learned – I never leave a bitch alone if there is a chance she might sneak off.

The first stage of labour may last for 24 hours but around 6 hours is more common. Bitches, more often than not, will give birth at night.

This is where the CCTV is really useful. The bitch is not constantly being disturbed by the helper going to check on her progress.

It will be obvious and visible when the bitch is having 2nd stage contractions and then she should not be left if at all possible.

So organising a chair, a good book and a cup of tea is a good plan!

24 hours old

Labour – Second Stage

Once the cervix is fully dilated the contractions increase in strength and become very noticeable. The first puppy usually takes the longest to be born so the rule of thumb is to be patient.

The contractions which deliver the puppies are incredibly powerful and you will see a bulge appear under the tail towards the vulva. The puppy will appear to be taking 'two steps forwards and one step back' in the birth canal.

The bitch will probably get up and lie down and it is not unusual for a puppy to be delivered whilst the bitch is standing.

Don't worry; it will not harm the puppy.

The normal presentation of the puppy is either feet and tail first, or head first. If the first one born is feet and tail first, it will be harder work for the bitch because the head is the biggest part of the puppy but coming last.

It may be necessary to assist the passage of the puppy by gently pulling the puppy down and in the direction of the stomach (down and forward as opposed to straight out) especially if the bitch is getting distressed.

Only do this when she is having a strong contraction. Be mindful of the fact that she may snap at you even though she knows you well – having the first puppy hurts (as a lot of women know…).

The bitch may yelp loudly when the first puppy is actually coming out – don't worry, this is normal and may happen as each puppy is born.

But, in my experience, after the second or third, as the birth canal has expanded with the birth of each puppy, she will stop yelping and get on with the job.

Once the puppy has been born it is vital that the membrane that is covering the puppy is removed to allow the puppy to breathe. The bitch will normally do this but in the case of a maiden (first time Mom) bitch or a bitch that is very heavy in pup and cannot get round to her rear end, the breeder should gently break the membrane and clear the puppy's nose.

Then bring the puppy and placenta, which will usually be still attached to the puppy, round to the front of the bitch. Most bitches will go about their work and stimulate the puppy to breathe by vigorous licking. She should tear the cord with her teeth and eat the placenta.

The bitch should lick and nose each puppy which encourages them to wriggle and exercise their tiny lungs. You will notice that she is not particularly gentle with her babies and will roll them around as she cleans them. This is natural and helps to stimulate the puppy.

If your girl does not tend to her puppy then you must help her.

Do not (as I've seen on many YouTube videos) leave a newborn puppy lying there *hoping* the bitch will take care of it.

It may die.

In this case the breeder must do all that is necessary to get the puppy breathing, i.e. remove the sac, tear the cord with your (clean) fingernails leaving about 2-3 inches attached to the puppy.

Then rub the puppy with a towel. Holding it in your hand with its head lowered a little; a vigorous rubbing along its back should make the puppy squeak and draw breath.

It is then breathing OK and you can leave it in the bed with the bitch. It is usual to see her responding to the cries of her puppy as the maternal instinct is triggered.

If the puppy is not breathing properly, perhaps it has been 'waiting around' for some time in the birth canal, then two drops of **Dopram** (available from your Vet and invaluable in a breeders 'toolbox') under the tongue can work wonders to stimulate the breathing reflex.

Another method to stimulate a puppy's breathing reflex is by using an acupuncture point which is located about half way down the crease on the nose between the nostrils. Using a blunt needle such as a darning needle, gently 'prick' the area a few times and you should see the puppy begin to breath.

If this is the bitch's first litter, she may react against the firstborn puppy and leap out of the bed to try to get away from it – after all she will have never seen anything like this tiny wriggly thing!

Gently ask the bitch back into the bed and reassure her. Most will settle down as more puppies are born. If she is not interested in the puppy, put it into a box with a heat pad to keep it warm until she is ready to accept it – which she will as more puppies are born.

It is OK to offer your bitch a drink of milk whilst she is waiting for the next puppy to be born, she may refuse but most are often really thirsty due to all the panting.

These puppies are warm and cosy with an infra red lamp helping to keep them warm

Labour – Third Stage

There is no need to apply anything to the cord if the bitch has chewed through it to separate the placenta from the puppy. She will keep the cord clean until it dries up and drops off – usually within 48 hours.

She will normally eat the placentas which will stimulate the release of the hormone oxytocin to help the womb to contract, and the milk to be let down. It also provides her with essential nutrients to help her through this strenuous time.

It is a normal process and should not be discouraged.

However, if she does not eat the placenta, remove it from the bed, place it in the bucket and remove it from the whelping area.

Occasionally the placenta does not arrive with the puppy, the cord having broken inside the bitch. This is not a cause for alarm as retained placentas are usually expelled at the end of the birthing process under the influence of a dose of oxytocin, administered by your Vet, to the help the womb to contract.

The bitch will then repeat the second and third stages of labour until all the puppies are born.

If she is very tired towards the end of delivering a large litter, she may push out a pup without noticing and neglect to remove the membrane. So don't leave her until you are certain that all the puppies are safely delivered.

The time between puppies will vary and sometimes bitches may rest for a couple of hours during the process.

As long as she is content and relaxed there is no need to worry.

However, if she begins contracting and becomes restless without a puppy showing, she may have a problem. Speak to your Vet.

It is important to monitor the time between each puppy to judge if a problem is occurring. A good plan is to record the time of the birth of each puppy along with its birth weight.

Sometimes it may be difficult to tell if she is finished having her babies or just resting.

It can be useful in this case to feel the abdomen for extra puppies. But an inexperienced person will find it difficult to tell if there are still puppies inside or they are just feeling the womb that is swollen.

It is a Good Idea for a Novice Breeder to Have an Experienced Person Available to Tell the Difference Between a Problem and a Normal Occurrence.

The following are signs of things not going to plan:

- More than 3 hours between puppies, even if the bitch is calm – ask your Vet for advice.

- If there are 20 minutes or more of strong contractions with a puppy visible, but not being delivered – ask your Vet for advice.

- 20 - 30 minutes or more of strong contractions, with no puppy visible – ask your Vet for advice

- A green/black discharge – ask your Vet for advice.

- Lots of bright red blood – ask your Vet for advice.

- A bitch that is very restless, crying or licking frantically at her behind – ask your Vet for advice.

It is crucial to respond *quickly* to any problems to save the lives of both the bitch and puppies.

If you don't know what to do – don't wait

Contact your Vet Immediately!

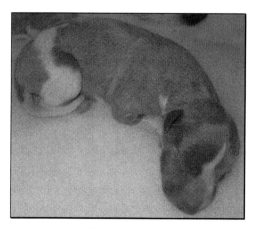

Whippet Puppy

More than three hours between puppies may mean that the bitch is simply restoring her calcium reserves so that the uterus can continue its work.

However, it may be that she needs an injection of oxytocin to stimulate further contractions – consult your Vet in this case.

A Vet will be required for any injection.

Before you go to the Veterinary surgery for the oxytocin, you could check your bitch to make sure that there isn't a puppy blocking the way through being wrongly positioned.

With CLEAN hands, check that either a nose or alternatively the feet and tail are presented first. If you can get hold of this puppy you can help it out by gentle traction when the bitch is contracting. Pull gently downwards and forwards towards her stomach.

It is important to get this puppy out as it is usually impeding the birth of other puppies whose placentas have detached from the wall of the uterus.

Sometimes taking her out of the bed and into the yard to 'empty' can help the puppy to move in the birth canal. But be vigilant – she may have a puppy whilst crouching to urinate or defecate.

Veterinary intervention is usually required if a puppy is stuck fast and, in order to save the remaining puppies and the bitch a caesarean section will have to be performed.

As each puppy is born it should move about in its search for food. They are guided to the teats by their sense of smell.

It is essential that each puppy suckles as soon as possible to get the colostrum which is full of essential antibodies to protect the babies from infection.

Sometimes a puppy may need to be helped onto a nipple. This requires practice as they don't usually want to be helped and have a tendency to squeal.

As long as the puppies are vigorous and lively it may be a good idea to leave them with the bitch for an hour or two before trying to attach them to a nipple. In my experience, they will usually find their own way to the 'milk bar' – but always help the ones that don't.

A puppy that has not suckled will not look as round or be as vigorous as its littermates.

The suckling of the puppies helps stimulate the natural release of the hormone, oxytocin which also lets more milk down and helps the uterus to contract as has been mentioned

A Very Relaxed Puppy (12 hours old)

Just Finished Feeding

Look at the shape of his tongue!

The sign that the whelping process is over is the bitch is seen to be relaxing and settling down to lick and care for her puppies. She might also just go to sleep.

Leave her for a few hours to get used to having all these tiny babies, then get someone to take her to 'empty' out whilst you quickly change the bedding. You may have to 'encourage' her to leave her puppies but almost all bitches will be relieved to be able to urinate.

When she is all clean and has relieved herself, it is important to let the bitch relax with her puppies without your interference which isn't needed for the moment.

Offer her a drink.

Milk is usually well accepted but don't worry if she doesn't eat much for the first day or so, as she has the nutrition from the placentas.

The First few Days

The first few days in the life of a puppy are crucial.

Most mothers will do everything that is necessary such as cleaning them, feeding them and keeping them warm and safe.

But a maiden bitch could easily trample or lie on the puppy if not watched closely.

A bar or 'pig rail' around the edge of the whelping box can greatly reduce the risk of this happening.

A Greyhound Mom and her 10 babies, just two hours old. (One of these tiny puppies went on to become a champion race dog!)

Some first time mothers can be very clumsy at this stage until she gets used the wriggling creatures that have just appeared.

It is also essential to ensure all the puppies are suckling and maintaining their strength.

Make sure that the puppies are either kept in a very warm room or have a safe heat source such as an infra-red lamp.

If using a lamp, it must be suspended over the puppies leaving enough room for the bitch to pass in and out without hitting it.

What to do after a Caesarean Section

The whelping box must be left warm so that the bitch and puppies can return to optimum conditions.

The bitch may wake up agitated after a Caesarean Section and may not relax with these wriggly things that are in her bed. This would apply particularly to a maiden bitch as she has never even seen puppies before.

If you are taking the bitch and puppies home immediately after the caesarean, ask your Vet for a sedative for her. There are many that the Vets have at their disposal.

Administer the sedative when you get her back into the bed and, as it takes effect, the puppies can be returned to the bitch. They should suckle immediately but any that are slow must be helped.

The continued sedation stops the bitch leaping up and staggering around risking injuring the new babies. She will come round gradually to the touch and sounds of the puppies and then, usually, she will take it all in her stride.

Observe her very carefully as she is waking up to ensure the safety of the puppies.

After a caesarean section the Vet will usually administer oxytocin as the bitch has not had the hormone stimulation of eating the placentas which helps with the milk production.

It is a good idea to give oxytocin again after a few hours, at levels to be discussed with your Vet, to ensure a continued milk production.

Weighing the puppies daily can help the breeder monitor each puppy, though the experienced breeder can easily identify a puppy that is not thriving.

In the first 24 hours it is normal for some puppies to lose a little weight, but after that there should be a definite gain every day, even if it is only a small gain.

Puppies that stay the same weight over a 24 hour period should be placed on the best teats, which are usually the ones nearer to the back legs.

Any puppy that loses weight should be monitored closely and supplemented with a bottle and puppy formula if necessary.

As a general guide, happy, well fed puppies will sleep for most of the day.

When they awaken they may make a little noise and will usually go for a feed. After about fifteen minutes or so they will fall back to sleep.

Puppies that continually cry are usually cold, hungry or in pain.

Therefore a happy litter is a quiet-ish one (a little squeaking and snuffling is nothing to worry about).

If the puppies are constantly crying, something is wrong – maybe the bitch has no milk or the house or kennel is too cold, but a Vet should be consulted in such circumstances.

What you should do if the bitch seems to have no milk

It is important to check that the bitch is producing milk by expressing a teat on a regular basis. The milk may not be profuse until around day two after she has given birth, but there should be some that you can see.

If there isn't or if she dries up after having milk, speak to your Vet about giving her oxytocin at 2 hourly intervals into the muscle at a dosage appropriate to her weight and breed. This should let the milk down. Keep giving the hormone as directed by your Vet, until a satisfactory milk production is seen. In the meantime you could try to locate a foster mother just in case.

Alternatively you should make sure that you have enough puppy formula and equipment needed for hand raising the litter.

However, in my experience, the oxytocin usually works.

Attention for the bitch after giving birth

Once she has had a rest she can be taken out in the yard to empty. She may need sponging down with warm water and drying off with towels as whelping can be a very messy process.

In addition to oxytocin to help cleanse the bitch, it is advisable to have your Vet administer an antibiotic especially if she has been checked internally. Your Vet will advise you on this.

Immediately after Giving Birth

Clear up the whelping area whilst the bitch is out in the yard. Remove all the wet bedding. Put clean VetBed™ or suitable bedding that is easy to wash and dry into the whelping box.

It is advisable to check the puppies whilst the bitch is out. If she is left in, their cries may distress her – even if she trusts you implicitly.

Check each puppy for limb abnormalities and particularly cleft palate.

This is where the palate is not joined and may be severe or very minor. In either case the puppy must be humanely put to sleep by the Vet as they cannot suckle with this condition.

The milk goes into the lungs and the puppy will eventually die.

The First Two Weeks

During the first two weeks the puppies are completely reliant on their mother. They can not see or hear as their eyes have not yet opened and their ears are still shut.

At this stage the biggest risks to the puppies are cold, hunger and infection. If a puppy becomes chilled it will become weak and is unable to suckle. When this happens the puppy will dehydrate very quickly as they have no body fat reserves.

They are unable to regulate their own temperature so it is crucial they don't wander off and get isolated from the rest of the litter. This is where the whelping box comes in useful, as it confines the puppies on all sides.

The puppies should sleep and suckle. Puppies usually wake as a group and the bitch will lick the puppies to stimulate urination and defecation.

Ten minutes spent watching the Mom and her puppies a few times a day will soon show you which puppies are the strongest and if there are any that are not as vigorous as they should be.

Check that the bitch is cleaning them all. A maiden bitch can be very awkward and slow to get the hang of the job.

The licking of the puppies by the bitch also ensures that their behind is kept clean and free from any build up of faeces that could prevent the puppies from passing motions.

This is a potentially life threatening situation.

If she isn't cleaning the puppies then it must be done using lukewarm water and cotton pads.

Try putting a little vegetable oil or butter on the puppy's behind to encourage the bitch to lick the puppy.

Not every whelping will go according to plan and you may lose one or two of the puppies – it happens. If you always have an experienced breeder or a Veterinarian on hand, you could prevent any mistakes that could be caused by your inexperience.

Remember to register the puppies with the Kennel Club.

With all the excitement and subsequent hard work involved with having a litter of puppies it is easy to forget to send off the registration form for the puppies. So, put a note in your diary to get this done in plenty of time so that each puppy has a registration form to go with him to his new home. Remember to include breeding restrictions on the registration papers. This ensures that any progeny from puppies that you sell will not be eligible to be registered at the Kennel Club. These restrictions can be lifted at a later date if the new owner wants to breed from his puppy – as long as the puppy is of the highest possible standard and has completed all veterinary tests to ensure that no inherited problems could be passed to the resultant progeny.

Looking after Mom

The bitch should be checked every day after whelping, as there are a number of key medical conditions that may arise. The most important and frequent of these are mastitis, eclampsia (milk fever) and uterine infection (Metritis).

Mastitis

It is important to check her teats for heat, soreness or possibly lumps developing. All bitches producing milk are at risk of developing mastitis, which is a bacterial infection of the teat itself. The affected teat becomes inflamed and hard, and may feel hotter than the other teats. Mastitis can occur suddenly and be very uncomfortable needing Veterinary treatment.

Symptoms of mastitis may include:

- Hard and hot teat.
- Milk from the infected teat becomes discoloured and thick
- Bitch may go off her food
- Bitch may appear lethargic

If these symptoms appear the Vet should be called immediately. Home help includes applying hot compresses and gently expressing the milk from the affected teat thereby releasing the pressure.

Alternatively get a strong puppy to suckle on the affected teat. It is advisable to get your Vet to administer antibiotics as a matter of course.

Eclampsia (Milk Fever)

This is usually associated with lowered calcium levels, and can occur even though post natal calcium supplementation has been carried out. This condition can occur up to 21 days after giving birth, especially if a large litter is involved.

Symptoms include anxiety and restlessness, shaking and shivering. The temperature is usually very high and the heart will be racing.

Call the Vet immediately as coma and death could be the outcome.

Uterine Infection (Metritis)

The bitch will have some discharge which could continue for several weeks depending on the bitch and will vary from reddish brown to a blackish green. It should not however be foul smelling or creamy in colour.

If this is noticed **Veterinary help will be required immediately.**

Metritis is an acute inflammation of the womb lining usually caused by a bacterial infection which may have been introduced during a manual examination of the birth canal or a retained placenta. This is a very good reason to administer antibiotics after the birth.

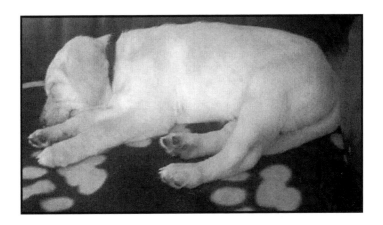

Looking after the Puppies

The puppies should be weighed daily to monitor weight gain but an experienced breeder can usually identify a puppy which isn't thriving.

As a general rule, puppies should double their birth weight in the first 8 days.

When asleep the puppies will twitch and jump. This is a perfectly normal reflex reaction called "activated sleep" and helps to develop muscles and exercise nerves.

The litter will tuck up to the mother's abdomen for warmth and will move away if it is too hot. If a heat lamp is used and is too warm the puppies will be scattered around.

If you feel that the whelping area is too warm, the lamp should be switched off and background heating such as an oil filled radiator should be used instead, as the overheated bitch could move away from her puppies to escape the direct heat of the lamp.

I usually hang the lamp to one side of the whelping box so there is room for the bitch to lie down away from the heat of the lamp.

Usually the puppies stay together in one or two groups near to a heat source – either the mother or the heat from the lamp. Be on the look out for a 'lone' puppy - it could have a problem.

Either the bitch is pushing it away because she knows there is something wrong or it isn't moving towards the bitch for milk.

The danger is that the lone puppy could get cold and become weak.

Visit regularly and place the weak puppy on a teat as often as you can.

Something as simple as this can sometimes save that puppy's life.

However it is sometimes an indication, especially if the bitch continues to ignore it, that there is a problem with that particular puppy.

When the puppies are handled they should feel warm and protest and tense up within seconds.

A cold puppy which remains limp and listless has a problem.

It may be sick.

It may not have been feeding properly or may even have a genetic problem.

A visit to the Vet will be required to determine the cause.

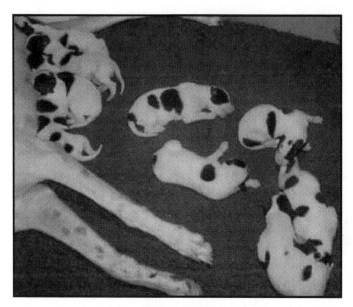

24 hours old

It is impossible to plan for every eventuality but where precautions can be taken it makes sense to do it.

Something that is often over looked is the regular trimming of the bitch's nails before the birth.

A bitch may stand on the puppies and will do less damage if her nails are short and smooth rather than long and sharp.

I had one maiden bitch who managed to stand on a tiny puppy, severing its ear. The puppy was fine – she just has a very tiny ear flap.

Most breeders will feed the bitch in the bed for the first few days after she has whelped. New Moms are usually very reluctant to leave their babies to feed themselves. Remember to offer a drink in her bed several times a day as well.

Most of the bitches that I have whelped down are fed in their bed for at least two days after the birth.

It is very important that dishes be scrupulously clean. It is advisable to reserve a set of dishes especially for the new Mom. By doing that, you are helping to guard against cross infection.

Along those same lines, it would be useful to limit visitors to the new mother and her babies. Parvo virus or other infectious diseases could be carried into the whelping area unwittingly, on the soles of the shoes.

If the puppies are constantly crying, then something is wrong and efforts should be made to determine the cause. Tiny puppies are very vulnerable and a whole litter can be lost in hours.

The bitch must be provided with fresh, clean water and will need to be fed as much good, high protein food as she will eat, as it is through the food that she will produce enough milk for her new puppies.

Water bowls should be placed outside the whelping area, as it has been known for a puppy to drown in a water bowl.

It may be necessary to take a good mother out on a leash into the yard a few times a day as she may be very reluctant to leave her puppies to go to the toilet.

Supplementing the diet with calcium after the birth is also a very good idea. The liquid form is the best as it is much more easily absorbed than the powder form.

Hand Rearing Orphan or Weak Puppies

There are a few situations where you will have to hand rear one or more puppies from a litter.

The bitch could die – it happens. There may be one or two weak puppies or she may refuse to have any of them anywhere near her, and you may have to hand rear a whole litter. This is very hard work, especially if it is a large litter.

In this situation it is much better for both the puppies and for the breeder if a foster mother can be found. The foster mother doesn't necessarily have to be the same breed but it does help if she is of a similar size breed to your puppy. Fostering a Yorkie puppy onto a Great Dane would probably result in the puppy being crushed by the other puppies.

To find a foster mother you could ask at the veterinary surgeries in your area or you could contact any breeding kennels to see if they know of anyone who has recently had a litter of puppies.

Most new mothers will not notice an extra one or two puppies and, in my experience, very few will object. It is advisable to have a foster mother that has given birth within a week of your bitch.

Before you introduce the new puppy, see if you can find a damp area within the whelping area of the foster mother where one of her own puppies may have urinated, then rub the new puppy with the damp bit so it will smell a little of the whelping area.

Then, when all the other puppies are feeding have someone hold the bitch's head whilst you put the new puppy or puppies onto the nipple to feed. If she is calm let her go, but watch her carefully. Most bitches will go about cleaning the new arrival and then treat it as she would her own.

If a foster mother is not available you should be prepared for a lot of sleepless nights! This applies if you are rearing one or two weak puppies or a whole litter.

Make sure that you have a tin of specially formulated bitch replacement milk – cows or goats milk will not do, it does not have the richness of bitch's milk. Your vet will be able to get this for you.

Follow the instructions on the tin *carefully* and make up the formula according to the instructions. You could get a bottle specially made for feeding orphan puppies but I usually use a syringe barrel to begin with.

Warm the recommended amount of formula to blood temperature, try a drop on the back of your hand to check it is not too hot.

The easiest way to feed a wriggling puppy is to wrap the bottom half of him in a warm towel, leaving his front legs free to 'paddle' as they would if feeding from his mother. Then, holding him in a position similar to how he would feed from his mother, begin to dribble the milk into his mouth.

Try and make sure that you get the recommended amount of milk into him at each feed. Do not try and give him extra – it is just as easy to kill a tiny puppy by over feeding as it is by under feeding.

A puppy will need feeding every two hours at first – night and day. So try and enlist a few helpers so you can get some sleep.

You must remember to stimulate him to urinate and defecate at each feed time. Recent studies have shown that a bitch will stimulate her puppies before they feed rather than after.

Use a cotton pad and some warm water to gently wipe around the abdomen and anus of the puppy until you get a result. Keep a record of when he urinates and defecates so that you know that he does not have some sort of blockage.

Make sure to dry him afterwards so that he does not become sore. Smearing a tiny bit of Vaseline on his tummy and anus can help a lot.

If you have been hand rearing a weak puppy, you could begin to try and put him back with his mother for short periods if he shows signs of getting stronger. Put him on a back nipple and check that he is suckling.

Watch the puppy's tail; it is a good indicator of whether or not it is getting a good feed. An erect, moving tail suggests that the puppy is being well fed

However, you may have to keep going with the bottle feeding until he is ready for weaning at around three weeks old.

Remember to increase the amount of milk that he is being fed according to his age/weight and the instructions on the can of formula.

It is possible that, even with all your careful attention, the weak puppy may still die. Don't despair; you have done all that you can and the puppy may have had some underlying problem that you weren't aware of. Be comforted by the fact that you did everything that you possibly could.

It is crucial at this stage that the puppy feeds every couple of hours, whether by himself or with help via supplementary feeding from the breeder.

If the puppy does not suckle or improve when being bottle fed it may need to go to the Vet for some subcutaneous (under the skin) fluids to be administered by injection in order to prevent dehydration.

To tell if a puppy is becoming dehydrated, pick up the loose skin on the back of his neck or 'scruff' and if it springs back quickly, he is fine. If, on the other hand, the skin stays up away from the body he is probably becoming dehydrated.

Speak to your vet as a matter of urgency as dehydration in a tiny puppy can very quickly become fatal.

Spend 5 minutes just watching mother and babies when you have to go into the whelping box. By doing this you will easily be able to observe a problem puppy.

During these first two weeks it is vital to keep the bedding clean and hygienic and to inspect the puppies at regular intervals.

It is also a good idea to gently handle the puppies, as it is strongly believed that handling at this stage greatly increases the puppy's ability to deal with the stresses of life later on.

The Third and Fourth Weeks

After about 10 days, the puppy's eyes and ears begin to open. They begin to wake up to their world and gradually start to explore. Their muscle tone and co-ordination is developing and they start to make their first attempts at walking.

At around 4 weeks they become more confident and begin playing with each other. They will begin to bark (then fall over...) and begin to try and run. At this age you can waste an awful lot of time just watching them play – it is so cute!

Four Week Old Puppies

At this time the bitch's milk production is at its maximum as are the puppy's appetites. She must be given as much high protein food as she can eat to allow her to produce enough milk for the puppies and to keep her own weight up.

It is also around this time that solid food may be introduced to the puppies as the bitch's milk will not be sufficient to satisfy them. Most breeders will begin with some soaked cereal in a flat dish.

You can also boil a little minced meat or possibly blend some soaked puppy kibble in a blender.

The food must be easy to eat and tasty.

Initially the puppies will walk all over the food and it may be necessary to gently introduce them to it by putting a little food on a finger and rubbing their mouths with it (I use a small plastic spoon used for human babies).

However, hungry puppies will very soon be eating enthusiastically.

Remove the bitch from the area whilst you feed the puppies as most will eat anything that you put down for the babies. As soon as they have finished let her in to clean up.

Most bitches will lick the puppies to remove any food that they will have inevitably smeared on themselves. Soon they will get the hang of eating from a dish and come running when it arrives.

This will keep the pressure off the bitch, who may have lost some weight due to feeding a litter of very demanding puppies.

Puppies, at this stage, spend a lot of time exploring their world and will begin escaping out over the side of the whelping pen if it is not high enough.

It may be necessary to provide them with a little puppy yard so that they can begin learning how to run and prepare for the outside world. They can be left outside for short periods provided the weather is warm and fine.

Once the puppies begin to eat solid food, the bitch will stop cleaning up after them. This is the age when puppies will learn the difference between their bed and where they go to the toilet.

It is important they are provided with other outlets away from their bed to go to the toilet. This way they learn to 'go' away from their bed.

I put newspaper just outside their sleeping area and most will learn to use the newspaper pretty quickly.

Leaving a piece of newspaper down that has been urinated on when you clean the toilet area, coupled with keeping their bedding clean and sweet smelling will help speed up the paper training process as they will smell the urine and soon learn where to 'go'.

Toys should be provided, as puppies have a tendency towards biting, chewing and causing general mayhem. At this time ropes and teddy bears are suitable toys.

Providing toys also prevents boredom.

These six week old puppies play outside with the 'multi-gym'. A few soft toys are hung up and suspended over the yard high enough so they don't get tangled in the ropes!

The Fifth Week onwards

As the puppies develop, they become more and more co-ordinated and their character and individual personalities begin to appear.

This is the main socialization period and is a very formative period for the puppy.

Therefore at this time, it is vital to expose them some of the things that they will experience in the future.

Things like people, noises, smells, etc, are some of the environmental factors they will encounter later on. The handling done at this stage will pay handsome dividends later in life by helping to produce a confident happy dog.

They can be weighed regularly and if you are intending to show them, they can get used to being 'stacked' and having their teeth inspected.

If the puppies are not handled regularly it may be very difficult to approach the scared puppy later on.

It is also very important to ensure that the puppies don't have any bad experiences at this stage.

The puppies should now be on five regular meals a day and it may be a good idea to begin weaning them off the bitch. This should be done gradually which will allow the bitch's milk to dry up naturally and also help prevent her from developing mastitis.

At 4-5 weeks, I would usually only let the bitch in to feed the puppies twice a day and leave her in with them at night.

However, some bitches will wean the puppies much earlier themselves and refuse to go in with them or she may even begin to snap at them if they try to feed.

If this happens, you should make sure that the puppies have plenty of fresh clean water available and feed them at least five times a day – depending on their age.

Puppies must have access to plenty of food. If a dominant puppy stands over the food and won't let the others near it, once he has had his fill and goes away to rest, the others will have the opportunity to eat. There must be plenty available for them all to eat.

However, using more than one dish is a good way to ensure that a dominant puppy can't chase the others away.

The food that the puppies eat should be gradually changed from soft and sloppy food to harder food. Be careful not to make any sudden changes in their diet which could cause digestive upsets and loose stools.

New foods should be introduced gradually over a few days to avoid any digestive upset.

At this stage, keeping the puppies area clean is a big and thankless task.

They tend to be very messy from 4 to 5 weeks old. Ideally a grass paddock or yard will be available to run about and toilet in.

It is vital to keep the sleeping area clean with fresh, sweet smelling bedding and toilet area clean in an effort to prevent infection.

Puppies can defecate more than four times a day; if you have 8 puppies this is a lot of waste. You must change the paper or clear up the 'emptying' area **at least** after every meal.

When the puppies are weaned they should be fed five times a day but this can be reduced to four times at around twelve weeks and then twice daily as they get to around six months.

Never leave uneaten food lying around. Remove it as soon as all the puppies have eaten. They will wander away when they have had enough.

But watch carefully to make sure that every puppy is actually eating, some seem to be eating well but are simply pushing it around the plate. The weight of the puppies will be a good indicator that all are eating their fill.

Ensure that feeding is done at the same times each day. All puppies thrive much better with a set routine.

At around 8-9 weeks old the puppies will be ready to go to their new homes.

Worming your Puppies

When the puppies reach two weeks of age they must be wormed for the first time.

Roundworm is a particular problem as it is passed through the bitch's milk to the puppies.

They are also passed back to the bitch as she cleans the puppies and eats their faeces.

At this age a liquid wormer is probably most suitable, as tablets can be difficult for a puppy to take.

Each puppy must be weighed and dosed **according to its weight on the day of worming.**

For as long as the bitch is still feeding the puppies, she should also be wormed at the same time; this will decrease the cross contamination of worms to her puppies.

Puppies are usually wormed fortnightly from 2 weeks up to 12 weeks of age then every month up to 6 months and every three months thereafter. They need to be wormed and dosed accurately with a product that will kill round and hook worms, at the minimum.

Puppies that are not wormed properly are not likely to thrive and develop to their full potential at this crucial stage in their life.

It is a good idea to rotate worm treatments using different brands (with different active ingredients) so the puppies don't build up a resistance to your chosen brand of wormer.

If you are at all unsure, please consult your Vet who will advise you on the correct wormers to use.

Nails

At the same time that you worm the puppies, it is important to clip their nails. Their nails are like tiny needles and the bitch may begin to avoid feeding them if their nails are scratching her as they feed.

I use human nail clippers whilst the puppies are still tiny; they are easy to handle when you are trying to holding a wriggling puppy.

So, as you can see, breeding a litter of puppies is not simply a matter of mating your bitch and then letting nature take its course. It takes time, money, dedication, patience and a great deal of courage along with lots of love to breed a healthy litter of puppies.

My Son's 9 Week Old Pet Yellow Labrador – 'Snoop Dog'

Moving to their New Homes

When the puppies are around 8 - 10 weeks old they will be ready to move on to their new homes.

Please make sure that each puppy will be going to a **permanent home**.

Do not allow a purchaser to take a puppy on the first visit. Let him go away and return a week or so later. It will give the purchaser time to decide if he is really ready to commit to the responsibility of owning a puppy.

Give a 'Puppy Pack' to each purchaser when they return to pick up their puppy.

What to Include in Your Puppy Pack:

1. **The Puppy's Pedigree, Registration Papers and a Receipt.**

You should supply a five generation pedigree which could include a photo of the entire litter and the Sire and Dam.

2. **Vaccination and Worming details for the puppy.**

Give details of any vaccinations along with details of the worming program that you have been using for the puppy. Advise when the next vaccination and worming is due.

3. **A Contract that Both Parties will Sign**

Include things like:

a) Any breeding restrictions.

b) Contact details for both the breeder and the purchaser and the date that the puppy is taken home.

c) If the purchaser encounters any problems with their puppy that he will get in touch with the breeder who will do his best to help.

d) The breeder will take back any puppy that the purchaser can not keep for any reason.

Every breeder should be responsible for any puppies that they bring into the world.

(see sample contract on p.117)

4) Information on Insurance

Include information on where to find pet insurance and why they should consider buying insurance.

5) A Weeks Supply of Food

Give the purchaser at least a full weeks' supply of the food that the puppy has been used to eating. It will give them time to change the feed to their preferred food gradually if they want to, without upsetting the puppy's digestive system.

6) Helpful Training Tips

I usually give my new owners a book or a printout of some easy tips for looking after a new puppy and along with some easy training tips.

There are other things that you could include such as a collar to fit the puppy, a feed dish or a piece of bedding from the whelping area so the familiar smell will comfort him in his new home etc. But, at a bare minimum, a responsible breeder would always include numbers 1- 5 above.

Be a Responsible Breeder – Do not breed puppies unless you are certain that you can find *GOOD PERMANENT* homes for them all!

Paula – My own Beautiful Pet Whippet

Helping a New Puppy to Join the Family

On the following pages there are some training tips for a new puppy owner.

You could write something along these lines and give them to your new owners to help them through the initial stages of owning a puppy. I usually give it to them when they have been to visit for the first time – **_before_** they take the puppy home!

Puppy Toilet Training

Now that you have chosen your new puppy, the very first thing that any new owner wants their puppy to learn is how to 'go' in the right place.

Puppy toilet training requires a great deal of patience for you and your family. You must always remember that your puppy is only a baby and, similar to a human baby, it takes time and a lot of repetition to teach him the correct place to 'go'.

To make the puppy toilet training process as easy as possible for both you and your puppy, it would be better if you were available to be with him as much as possible whilst you are going through the toilet training stage.

As soon as your new puppy arrives home, let the introductions wait and take him straight outside to the place you have decided will be his toilet area.

Stand with him and, if you want to use a 'trigger' word, say this to him as he performs then praise him for doing the right thing. My trigger word is 'quickly' and my dogs know, if I take them outside and use the trigger word, that it is not playtime and they know to 'go'.

You should use puppy training pads or even old newspaper to place near the back door overnight so, if he can't wait, he can 'go' on that instead of the kitchen floor.

Once your puppy has been introduced to his new family, the next step in making his education easier on you both is to establish a routine – again, much like a human baby.

A regular feeding routine will make toilet training him much easier as his digestion gets used to regular food and he will 'go' on a regular basis.

When toilet training; it is your responsibility to teach your puppy where to 'go'. There will be accidents, but there must be no reprimands unless you catch him actually doing it – not even 5 seconds later.

If you do 'catch him in the act', simply say 'no' in a low growling tone then take him outside to your chosen toilet spot. Praise him when he 'goes'.

Puppies and dogs do not have a guilt emotion, they live for now.

He will not understand why you are upset with him because, for him, that moment has gone. He will not understand why you are pointing to a puddle on the floor and telling him he is bad.

So realise that if he has an accident, **it is *your* fault** not his, because you didn't watch him and notice that he wanted to 'go'.

Take him outside regularly, at least every hour whilst he is still very young.

Never, *EVER*, rub his nose in it if he has an accident – that is downright cruelty!

Always take him outside *immediately,* when he wakes up from a nap and as soon as he has finished his feed. Follow the same procedure as when he first arrived home and always stay with him during this training stage so you can praise him for doing the right thing.

It may be tedious but it considerably shortens the process because he gets a positive reaction from you, which is really all a puppy wants – to please you.

Puppy toilet training is a very trying time for you and your family, but if you are consistent and take him out at regular intervals, it shouldn't take more that a couple of weeks before your puppy is clean in the house. However, most puppies do not have complete control until they are at least 16 weeks old.

There will be the occasional accident but hang on in there, your persistence will pay off in the end.

Puppy's first check up

Bringing your puppy home

There are a lot of things to consider before you bring your new puppy home to share your world.

Now you have chosen your puppy you need to organize one or two basics before you bring him home. You will need:

- Somewhere for him to sleep that will be his own secure 'den' – a crate is a good option.
- Dishes that will only be used for your puppy – don't buy tiny ones if he is going to grow into a large dog.
- Dog food.
- Collar and lead. *Definitely not* a chain collar – a lightweight leather one is much kinder.
- Toys – old socks with a knot in the middle, an old slipper, a soft toy for him to cuddle at night, a hide chew etc.
- Puppy training pads or even just save your old newspapers to use to help toilet train your new puppy.
- Cleaning equipment for cleaning up any 'accidents'.
- Be aware of where your local veterinarian is located and write down the phone number.

- Choose a name for him *before* he comes home, so you can begin using it as soon as he arrives. He will soon begin to answer to his new name if you use it every time you speak to him.

When you go to pick up your new family member (puppy), do so as **early in the day as you can**. It will give him all day to settle in before you leave him to go to bed.

If you have a car crate it would make the journey much more pleasant for both puppy and you. If not, and he will be travelling on someone's lap, be sure to take regular towels, paper towels and garbage bags to mop up any vomit etc, should he become car sick.

When you arrive home, take him straight out into the spot you have chosen for him to do his business. Stand with him and praise him enthusiastically if he 'goes'. Don't be upset if he has a few accidents

When you take him inside the house, try not to encourage too much excitement – remember he is only a baby.

Right from the moment your new puppy arrives home, you and all of your family should begin teaching him how to behave within your family 'pack'.

This will make his transition from living with his siblings to being an 'only child' much easier.

Once he realizes that he is secure and safe within your 'pack' he will settle down quickly and easily.

Buying your first puppy is very rewarding and, with some forward planning, his arrival should go without a hitch.

Early Puppy Socialization

Socialization should begin as early as possible in your puppy's life. Early puppy socialization will help your puppy adapt easily to the many different experiences he will encounter during his lifetime.

Even when your puppy is still at the breeders, it is advisable for the breeder to handle all the litter as often as the mother is comfortable with. Most bitches don't mind their owner picking up the tiny pups. However, not all will be happy with a stranger handling their babies.

We handle our puppies daily as we check them for any problems. So, as they open their eyes and begin to be able to hear what is going on around them, they are not at all fearful of humans.

As you have taken on the responsibility of a new puppy, it will be your job to expose him to as many different experiences as you can. Make sure he feels safe in any new situation that you place him in. I don't mean that you should constantly tell him he is a 'good boy' – this should be reserved for when he is showing signs of being confident and happy in a given situation.

If he is obviously frightened with any new experience, you should try to 'jolly' him along with an encouraging voice, showing him by your example that there is nothing to be afraid of.

If he is not comfortable with a situation, try asking him to do something that you know he can do, like 'sit', then praise him lavishly. This will take his mind off the scary stuff and the next time he encounters it, he will only remember the praise – not the fear.

Try to expose him to situations involving other dogs, children, vehicles, cycles, cats, busy roads and anything else that you think he may encounter later in life. It is important that you always remain calm as he will pick up on your feelings and react accordingly.

If you neglect the early puppy socialization, your sweet little puppy could grow up to be a fearful, nervous adult.

Fearful dogs could react aggressively to any situation that they feel is threatening.

Failure to understand the need for early puppy socialization combined with the lack of early (or in some cases – any...) training is a contributory factor to many families dumping their adolescent dog at the local animal shelter because he is unruly and showing signs of aggression.

Early puppy socialization will ensure that your pet will grow up to be confident, happy and most importantly, permanent, member of your family.

Another great idea when you have a new puppy is to ask around to see where you can go to a puppy training class. Your Vet is a good person to ask, if they don't know they will be able to tell you who to ask.

Puppy Training

You may not have a lot of time to teach your puppy to do elaborate circus tricks but every puppy needs some basic puppy training. For your pups safety and your sanity, start with these three.

A few minutes a day is all that is needed to start – your puppy is still a baby so his concentration doesn't last long!

1. Sit

This is usually quite easy to teach your puppy as long as you work with his natural movements. There is no need to push his bottom to the ground whilst saying 'sit'.

Instead, watch him as he is going about his business and, the minute you see him begin to sit down, say '[his name], sit'. Then praise him lavishly, you could even give him a treat.

Do this every time you see him sitting down and before you know it, he will sit when you ask him to.

2. Wait

For this you will need your puppy on a leash and you should have some treats in your pocket.

Walking briskly along you should stop in your tracks whilst saying 'Wait' in a firm voice.
Obviously, your puppy will stop as you have him safely on a leash, so bring him to your side.

When he is standing calmly next to you (probably with a puzzled look on his face...), give him a treat whilst saying 'good boy'. I use treats for this exercise as lavish and enthusiastic praise promotes excitement and I prefer a calm approach whilst teaching this exercise on the road.

Repeat when you have to wait to cross a road or where you have to stop for a few seconds.

You will be surprised at how quickly he learns this simple request.

When he has mastered this on a leash, take him to a safe place where you can let him have some free time and let him play for a minute or two.

Then, when he is close enough to hear you, say his name and 'Wait' in the same tone you used previously.

If he ignores you, just try one more time then go back to the leash for a while to reinforce the request.

However, if you have been thorough in your on-leash training he should stop and wait for you to go to him.

Then you can give him a treat and praise him lavishly.

This one request, learned properly could save your new friends life!

3. Recall

This simple puppy training exercise will make your life so much easier once you and your puppy have mastered it.

Take your puppy to a safe area where you can let him off his leash. Let him play for a few minutes, then call him to you with enthusiasm.

If your puppy runs away from you, don't chase him – he'll think it's a new game. Instead, ignore him and walk the other way. Say his name just once to get his attention but keep walking.

If you have established yourself as the 'pack leader' before you try this, he will follow you.

When he returns, always praise him and let him loose again. Don't put the leash on him the first time he returns, wait until you call him the second time then give him a treat and put the leash on him.

He will (eventually) see that you don't always intend to stop his playtime and when you put his leash on it is always good.

Never punish your pup if it takes a while for him to return to you – he will associate coming back to you with bad stuff.

Always praise him for returning, even if it takes ten minutes!

A trick that I have used to get a puppy to return when he is proving hard to catch is to sit on the floor and pretend to be looking at something really interesting. Most can't resist coming to see what you are doing.

Crate Training

Before you bring your new puppy home, consider getting a dog crate. Training him to accept the crate as his own space is easier if your puppy is introduced to his crate on arrival at your home.

Before your puppy arrives, put the crate in a suitable place in your home and put your chosen bedding in place, along with a soft toy.

I put mine in my sitting room so my dogs can see what is going on, but from their own private 'den'. I place a cover over the crate to make it a bit more private, just leaving the door area uncovered.

Crate training should begin as soon as your puppy arrives home. Crate training is very simple.

Leave the door open to begin with and show him how to get in by putting him gently inside and giving him a treat when he is inside; leave the door open and allow him to come out if he wants to.

Keep encouraging him to go in and reward him if he goes in voluntarily. After he has been in a few times on his own, put him in with something nice, like a bone or a dog chew, and shut the door.

However, your puppy may howl a little at first when you shut him in but he will very soon get used to it. At feed times put his food bowl inside the crate and shut him in whilst he eats (but remember to take him outside as soon as he has finished).

Only give him treats inside the crate, training him to go inside before you give him any treat, he will soon begin to associate being in his crate as a good thing.

Another bonus to feeding him in his crate in the early days is that dogs rarely soil their own sleeping area, so he will try and 'hold it' until you take him outside.

Crate training your puppy is an advantage to both puppy and family. A crate is great for when your puppy gets over excited and needs time out to calm down.

It is also invaluable if you have young children, your puppy can be put in his crate to stop the children from encouraging him to be silly.

Also if you have to go into another room you should never leave a puppy and small children unsupervised. So always put him safely in his crate.

If your puppy jumps up at a small child and knocks him over, the puppy will be blamed for hurting the child, when in reality it is the fault of the family for not teaching him the right way to behave or not supervising him until he learns the right way to behave.

Crate training your puppy is invaluable for helping to potty train him; as well as being a great way to keep your puppy out of harms way if you need to go out for a short while and cannot take him with you.

You can be sure that he will not get himself into trouble whilst you are away – nor will he be able to trash your home!

More Puppy Training Tips

Being a responsible dog owner is not just a matter of getting a puppy and letting it loose in your life. It is all about helping your puppy to integrate into your household smoothly and with as little stress and confusion as possible.

Here are a few more puppy training tips you could use to help your puppy to settle quickly into your family:

- Decide before you get your new puppy what boundaries you will set for him. For instance, will he be allowed on the furniture? If not, then make sure everyone in your family knows to put him gently on the floor every time he tries to climb on the sofa. No words are necessary; remain calm yourself, put him on the floor without even looking at him. When he remains on the floor, then praise him well.

- Where will he sleep? Decide on your new puppy's sleeping arrangements before he arrives home. Make sure he has a bed of his own so he has a place to go to if he needs to sleep or just to escape from the children. A crate is a good solution because you can close the door to keep him safe if you have to leave him for a while.

- Before he arrives, decide on the spot in your yard where he is to go to the toilet. Take him regularly to that spot and praise him when he 'performs'. It will take a few weeks for him to become 'clean' but you should persevere, it will be worth it in the end.

- If he has an accident in the house, you should clean the spot with soda water; it will remove lingering smells which would encourage him to use the same place again.

- Teach him not to jump up at you by ignoring him and turning away every time he launches himself at you. Only pay him any attention if all his feet are on the floor. If you do this every time, instead of reacting by screeching or shouting, he will soon get the message. Puppies hate to be ignored.

- Don't allow him to bite or nibble at you. When he was with his littermates all their games involved biting and chasing. It will be your job to show him that the rules are different in his new home. Be gentle – no smacking. Simply 'yelp' as soon as his teeth come into contact with you, then turn away. If he carries on, turn your back on him and ignore him.

Do not speak to him or look at him until he calms down, then ask him to do something you can praise him for – like 'sit'.

- Decide with your family how you are going to train your puppy. What words will you use? What things do you want to teach him? If you decide, as a family, to stick to a certain set of words that you will use, it will cause much less confusion for your new puppy and he will learn more easily.

The most important puppy training tip I can offer is – be consistent so your puppy can easily learn what is expected of him.

Most puppies only want to please you, so make your training is simple for him to understand, be kind and praise him lavishly when he does the right thing.

How to Stop Your Puppy Chewing

Have you seen the damage a small puppy can do when he gets hold of one of your best shoes? You can be sure that you'll never be wearing that pair again!

It is a puppy's natural instinct to chew things, just as a baby puts things in his mouth. One of the reasons that both baby and puppy chew things is to ease the discomfort of teething.

The simple way to stop your puppy chewing things he's not supposed to is by making sure he has his own stuff that he is allowed to chew.

Remember to put all your things out of your puppy's reach so he can't chew your favourite slippers etc. However, even chair legs are fair game to a bored puppy.

In order to discourage this destructive behavior and stop your puppy chewing random bits of your furniture, you should crate train him as soon as he arrives at your home. This will save a lot of frayed tempers and chewed furniture if you have to leave him alone for any reason.

Whilst you are home with your puppy it is important to teach him that he is only allowed to chew his own toys.

If he begins to nibble at anything that is not allowed, simply remove him from the area and give him something of his own to chew on.

Distract him from the wrong thing by making the right thing seem really interesting. You can tell him 'no' or 'leave' as you are removing your best Jimmy Choo shoe from his mouth, then exchange the forbidden object with a soft toy or a chew from your puppy's own toy collection.

But remember if you leave your things lying around, it is fair game to your puppy. Teach all the family to put their things away if they don't want them chewed by their new family member.

Prevention, in this case, is better than cure!

If your puppy is a persistent offender, always put him in his crate with something nice before you leave him alone.

A Kong™ stuffed with peanut butter and put in the freezer for a few hours will give him something to do and the coolness of it will soothe his sore gums.

It is not easy to stop your puppy chewing but with vigilance you can, at least, stop him from destroying your house and property.

Introducing a Second Dog into Your Family

Any family who enjoys dogs will undoubtedly want more than one. Normally the addition of another dog would not cause a problem but that is not always the case. Some dogs are very territorial and protective of their family which could result in problems when you try to introduce a new dog.

The sex of the dog you want to bring into the family is not really important if you make sure that both animals are neutered. However, if it is a tiny puppy you should make sure that you remember to get it neutered when it is old enough.

Now that you have decided to introduce a new puppy into your house, make sure it is not your dog's favorite person in the world that carries the new pup into the house.

Take the puppy straight outside to 'go' then bring him into the house and allow your dog to check him out. Grown up dogs will usually understand that he is just a baby and will set about teaching him some manners. He will tell the puppy off if it oversteps the mark, just keep an eye on them but don't interfere unless you have to.

Never leave them alone together until you are sure that the puppy understands that your grown dog gets to set the rules.

Quite often you will find an old dog gaining a new lease of life when you introduce a puppy into the household and that's great, but if your older dog doesn't want to be bothered with a boisterous pup make sure there is somewhere quiet that the older dog can retreat to if he finds it all too much.

Leash Training

Leash training your new puppy can begin as soon as he has settled into your home. But remember to conduct your initial leash training around your own property until he has had his vaccinations.

Leash training is a very important part of training any new puppy. You need to know that your dog is safe when you venture out in to the big wide world with him for the first time.

Never allow him off the leash in any public place unless you are 100% confident that he will return when you ask him. Distractions, such as other very interesting dogs, will severely test your recall training. Better to be safe than sorry.

The easiest way to begin leash training is to put a soft leather collar on him, (no chain collars) he will probably scratch at this foreign object that is round his neck, but all puppies get used to it soon enough.

When fitting a collar, adjust it so that you can comfortably fit two fingers between the collar and dog. Check the collar regularly as puppies grow fast and the collar that once fitted perfectly will soon become very tight and uncomfortable.

Once he gets used to the collar, attach a short, leather or webbing leash and allow him to trail it around behind him. Always supervise him when he has the leash attached as he could get tangled up and frighten himself.

After a couple of times of him trailing the leash around behind him, it's time to attach yourself to the other end of the leash. The next time you clip the leash to his collar, keep hold of it.

Then you should follow him around, putting as little pressure as you can on the collar and leash. If he wants to dash off in front – you follow, if he wants to stop – you stop.

Just a few minutes each time is enough to begin with. Before unclipping the leash from his collar, try and wait until he is walking next to you (even for a couple of seconds...), then praise him and let him go.

Obviously all this is taking place on your property, so he can't dash off in to the path of a car!

The next step in leash training is to show him how to walk next to you without pulling.

Once he accepts the leash and walks confidently with it on, you would begin to ask him to walk next to you by giving a very quick tug sideways on his leash to remind him that you are there.

Then hold his leash in such a way that he can not walk in front, every time he tries to pull ahead, the short sideways tug on the leash will remind him that you are the leader – not him.

No verbal communication is necessary; just make sure that you remain calm and confident all the time.

Before you know it, the initial leash training is done and your puppy will be trotting confidently by your side as you go out on your walks together.

5 Simple Rules for Teaching Your Dog Not To Jump Up

There is nothing more annoying than an unruly dog that launches himself at you every time he sees you. Even a very small dog becomes a nuisance if he continues to jump up and down.

Each time you tell your dog 'no' or 'down' or whatever, you are giving him exactly what he is demanding – attention! If you are to be 'the leader' in your dog's eyes, it is you who should decide when he gets attention.

My own children (years ago!) could not understand why our nutty Labrador never jumped up at me and waited calmly until I greeted her, but always greeted them by leaping up at them and tearing round the house.

It was because they never enforced any rules in regard to acceptable dog behavior.

This was before the days of The Dog Whisperer phenomenon, but I was, albeit unwittingly, using the 'pack leader' mentality and ignoring her until she was calm.

In order for your dog to learn what is expected of him quickly and easily; everyone in your family needs to enforce The 5 Rules for teaching your dog not to jump up.

The procedure for this is very simple – although it may take a few weeks before your dog understands what is expected of him.

THE RULES

1. When you arrive home or anytime you have been away from your dog, ignore him until he is calm.

2. Each time he jumps up at you, turn your back and walk away.

3. Absolutely no talking to him.

4. Remain calm yourself.

5. When he is calm, ask him to sit then pet him and tell him how good he is. Reward him for sitting and remaining calm.

He will eventually learn that only calm behavior gets him any attention.

That's it – Simple but very effective if everyone in your family sticks to these 5 rules.

Always remember that your puppy can only concentrate for short periods of time. So make your training sessions short and fun.

He is only a baby and will really enjoy being with you – all he asks for is food, water, warmth, comfort, direction (training) and, most importantly, LOVE!

The Best Part about Owning a Dog...

... is the way he will come over to see you, for no reason, just to let you know you're important to him

... is the way he is always ready to lick the jelly off your nose...

... is the way he looks into your eyes and finds

contentment in simply being near you

... is the way he will run all over the yard, fetch a soggy tennis ball and bring it back to you as if to say "look mom, it's all have, but it's yours

... is the way he wakes you up in the morning by pushing his cold wet nose in your ear and snuffing loudly

... is the way he shreds toilet paper all over the house, because it's fun even though he knows he shouldn't

... is the way he's sure he can catch the ducks in the lake today...

... is the way he comes over to you when he is sad

... is the way he wedges himself near you when you are sad and pushes all others away, to console you with his love

... is the way he pounces on crickets in the backyard

... is the way he looks perplexed when the crickets escape

... is the way he is terrified of the evil pink hula hoop

... is the way he doesn't mind how much of that horrid perfume you're wearing just because it was a gift from a relative who's visiting

... is the way he doesn't care about bad hair day or overdue bills

... is the way he loves you, even when you are impatient with him and have no time this morning for a game of tug-a-war

... is the way his coat feels like liquid silk under

your fingers

... is the way he finds wisdom beyond words

Unknown

"If you can look at a puppy and not feel love and affection – you must be a cat..."
~ Author Unknown

Agreement between Breeder and Purchaser

Breed of Puppy _____ Sex _____
Name of Puppy _____
Date of Purchase _____
Breeders Address _____.
Phone No. _____.
Purchasers
Address _____.
Phone No. _____

THIS PUPPY IS SOLD AS A PET - NO PROGENY CAN BE REGISTERED

The Breeder agrees to take back ownership of the puppy and refund any monies paid if the puppy, on veterinary inspection, is proven to have any illness or disease originating from the breeders premises. **This will apply for 5 days from the date the puppy is picked up from the Breeder.**

The Breeder will be available at any reasonable time of the day to answer any questions that the purchaser may have regarding the health and training of the puppy.

The Breeder agrees to take and re-home the dog at any time in its lifetime should the purchaser no longer be able to keep it. This will be at no expense to the purchaser.

The Purchaser agrees to have the puppy checked by a Vet within two days of picking him up from the breeder. S/he further agrees that vaccination and worming are carried out at the appropriate times as recommended by the veterinary and to provide any veterinary treatment that the puppy will require throughout its life.

The Purchaser agrees to return the puppy within 14 days for a refund (less an administration fee) if, for any reason s/he cannot keep the puppy. After 14 days any refund will be at the complete discretion of the breeder.

The Purchaser agrees to return the dog to the breeder for re-homing at any time during the dog's lifetime if s/he can no longer keep it.

The Purchaser agrees to have the puppy neutered as soon as recommended by the Vet. (Delete if not appropriate)

Breeder Signature_____

Purchaser Signature_____

Always Breed
Responsibly –
There are enough
unwanted dogs in
the world!

Printed in Great Britain
by Amazon